Mind's Eye Geometry

Ivan Moscovich

The three pairs of common tangents to three
circles appear to meet on a straight line.
Is this a coincidence or does it always happen?

TARQUIN PUBLICATIONS

Mirror Flips

In your imagination, flip each of these four pieces
about their mirror lines.
What shape do they then make?

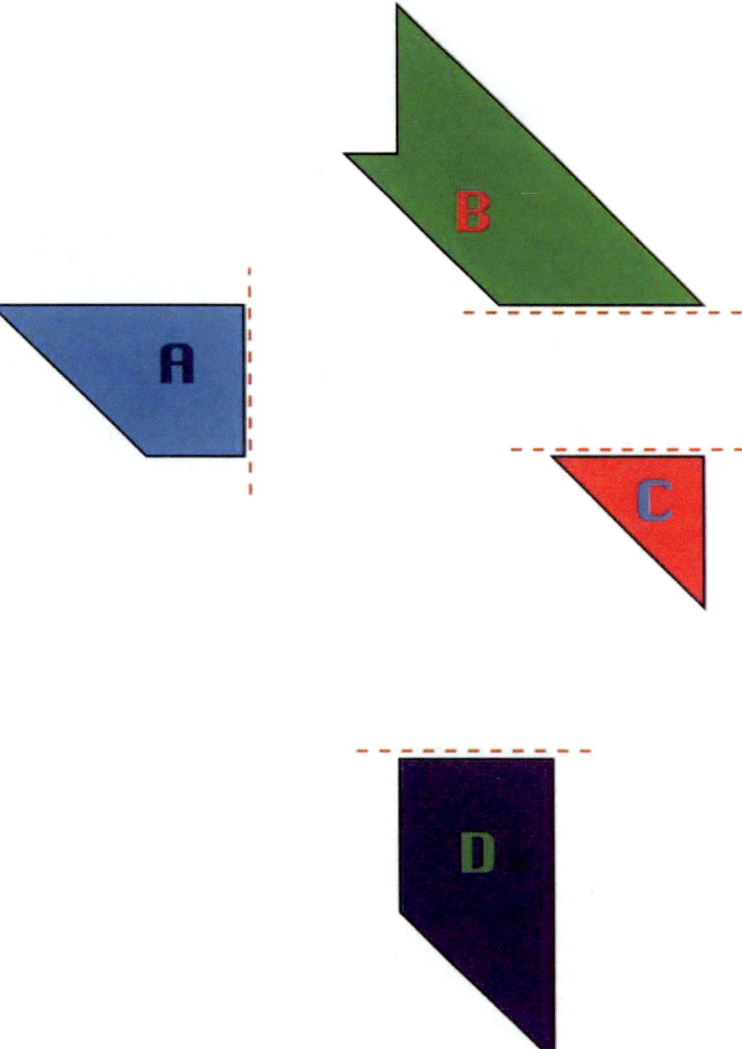

Use the 'Puzzle Proof Cut-out' from page 27 to verify your solution.

Lift Off

2

Each of these frames can be lifted off one at a time so that none of them disturbs any other.
In your mind's eye, can you find the correct order of working?
When you do, the letters on the frames spell out an appropriate word beginning with M.

Use the 'Puzzle Proof Cut-out' from page 27 to verify your solution.

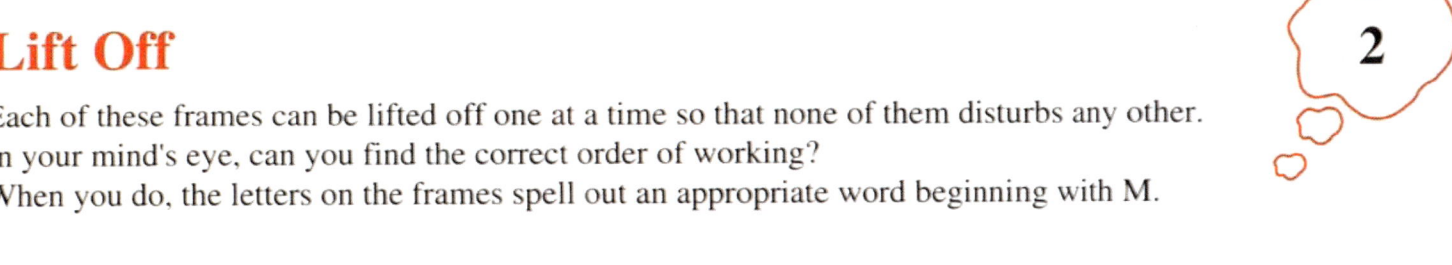

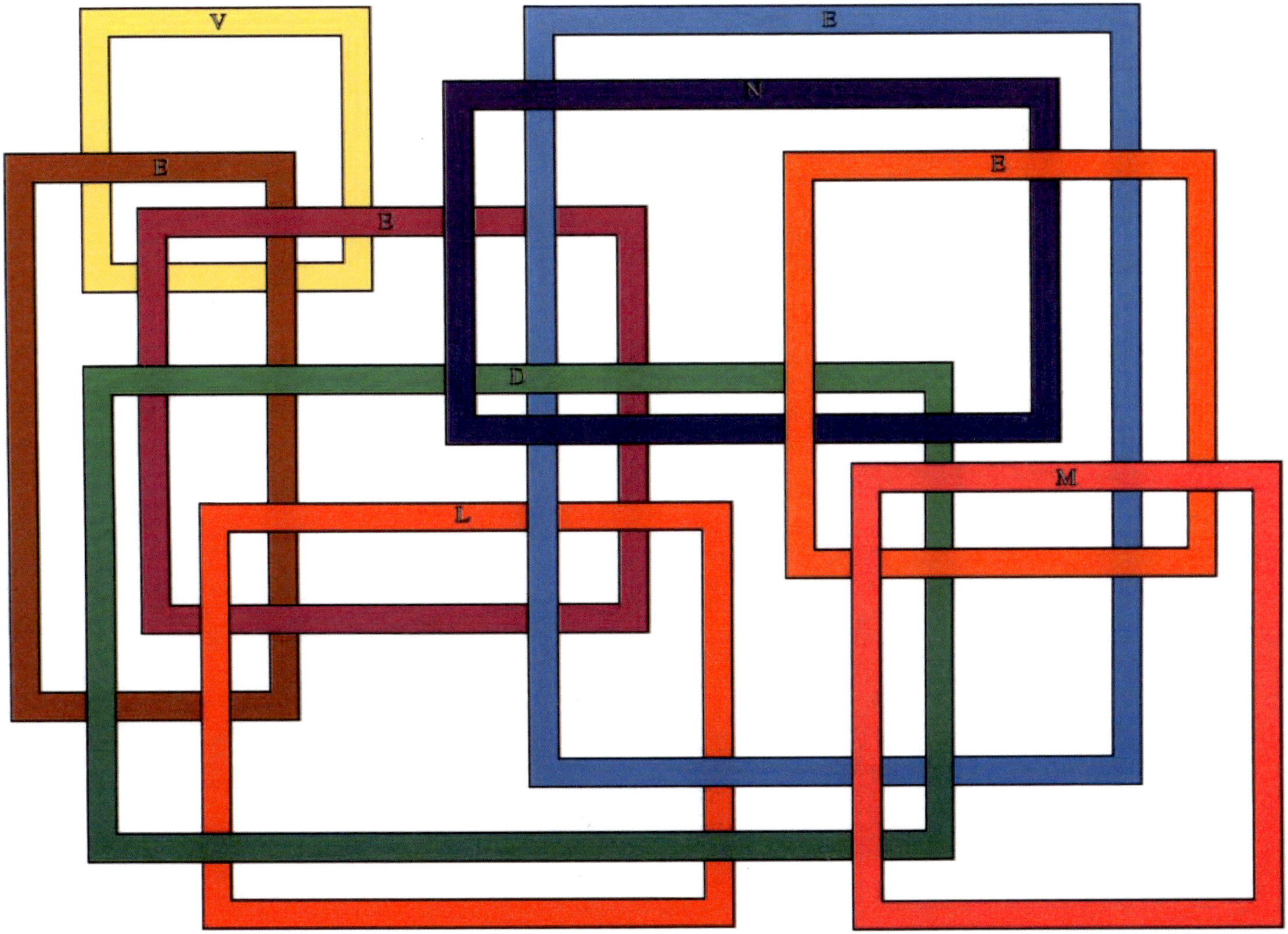

Two by Two

In your mind's eye, arrange these four tiles into a 2 x 2 square
so that they make a complete picture.
What well-known geometrical property does it illustrate?

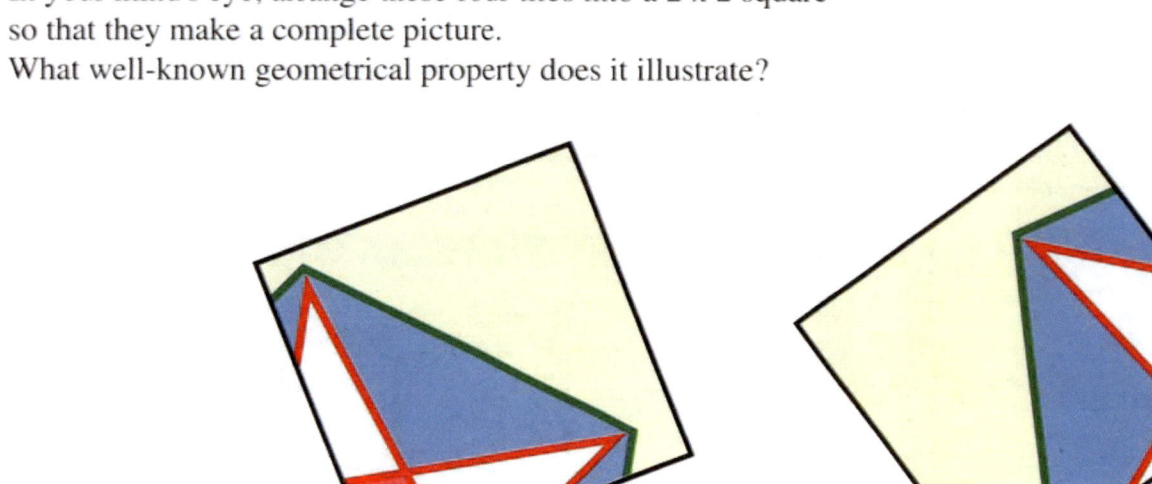

Use the 'Puzzle Proof Cut-out' from page 29 to verify your solution.

Sixth Sense

Triangles radiating from the centre divide each edge of every square into six equal lengths. They are coloured with six colours, one of each along every edge. In your mind's eye, can you work out which colour will form the continuous zig-zag pattern illustrated at the centre? Exactly four of the squares have to be rotated about their centres before it will work. Which?

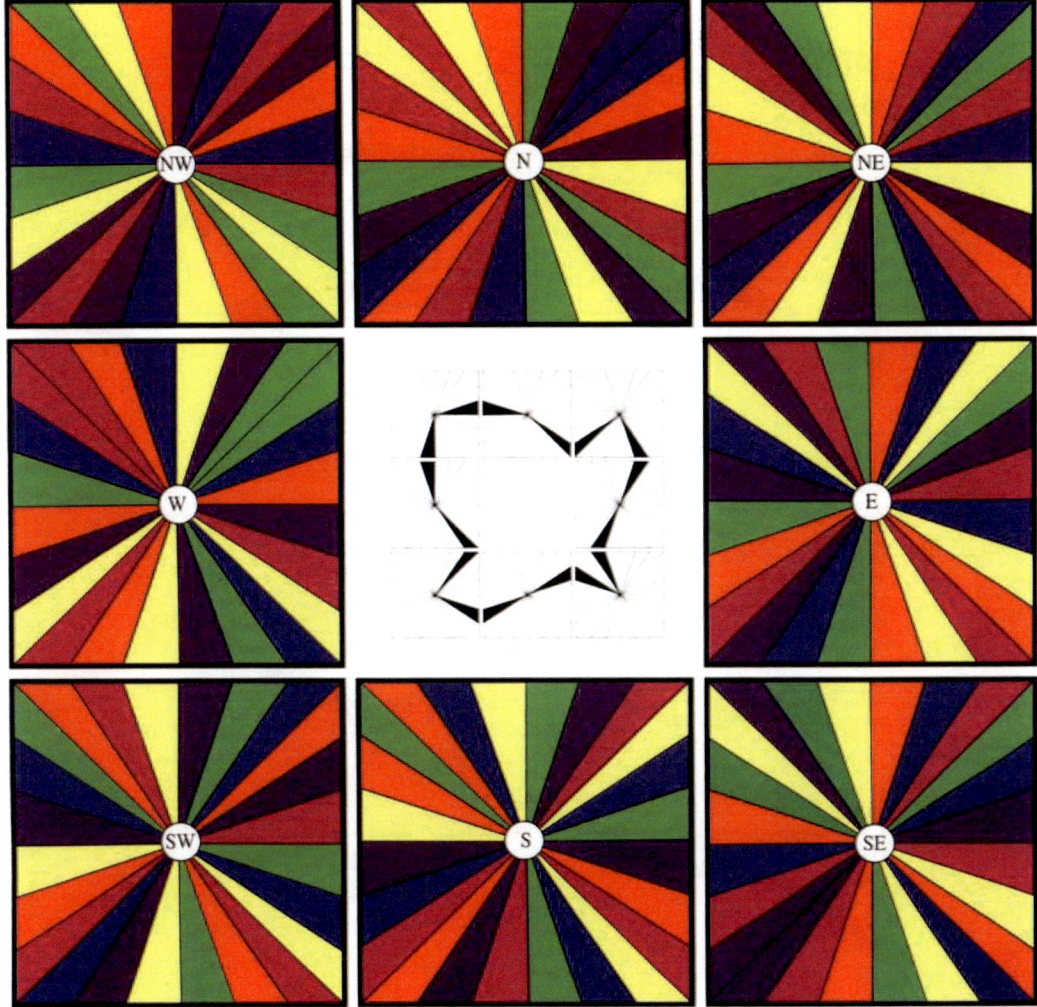

1. Green
2. Yellow
3. Orange
4. Pink
5. Purple
6. Blue

Polygon Bracelet

These eight linked regular polygons will pull out into
a circular shape to make a lucky charm bracelet.
In your mind's eye, can you work out what is special
about the polygons that are opposite each other?
Can it really be a lucky charm?

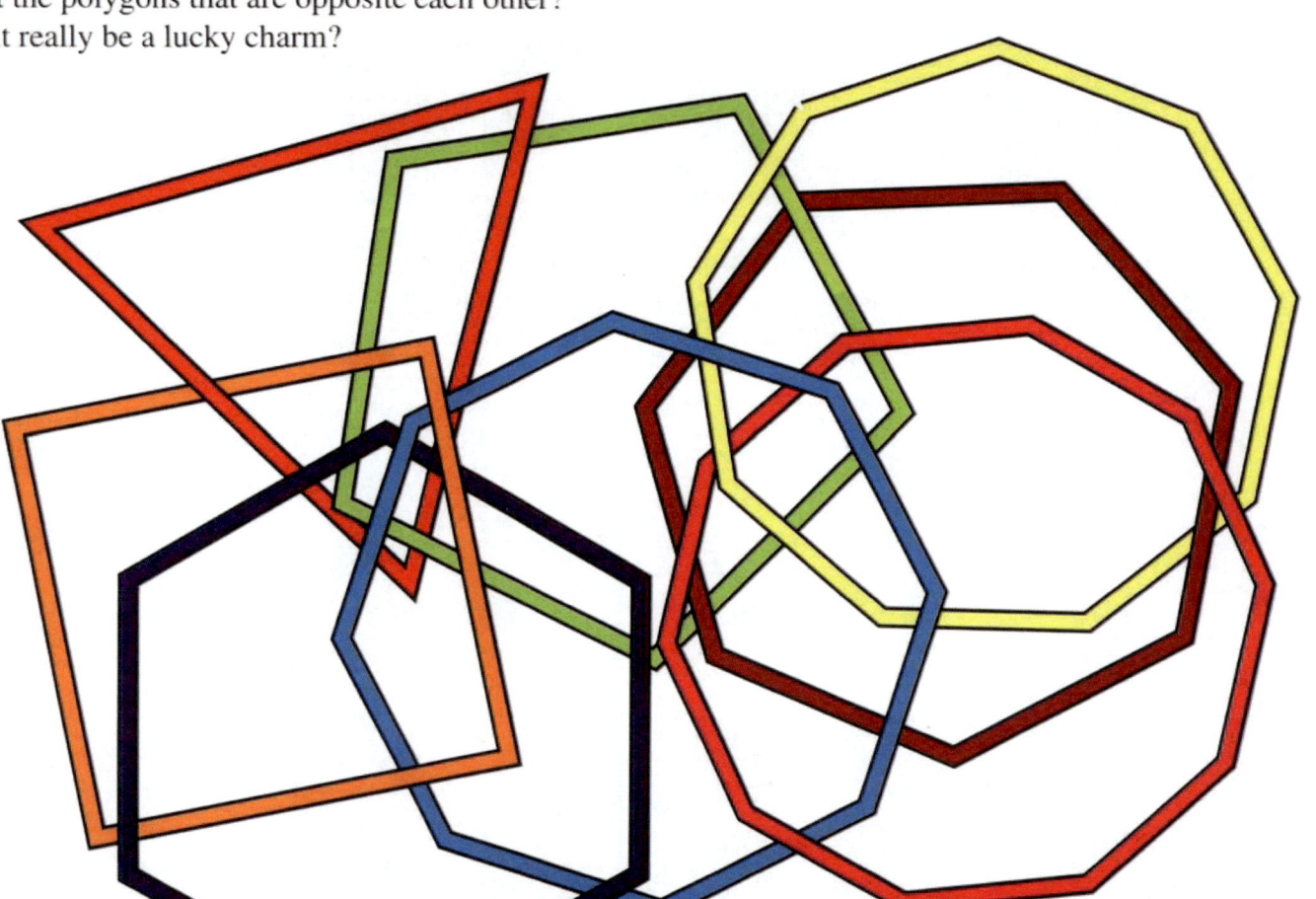

Use the 'Puzzle Proof Cut-out' from page 29 to verify your solution.

Triangle Count

A white mask of unknown shape has been placed over
a collection of equilateral triangles.
What is the least number of triangles there could be?

Take Three, Six or Ten

It is easy to arrange coloured dominoes to make a rectangular pattern, but harder to see how dominoes can be arranged to make a particular finished design.
In your mind's eye, can you make each of these three patterns by taking and arranging three, six and ten dominoes from the set shown below?

TAKE THREE

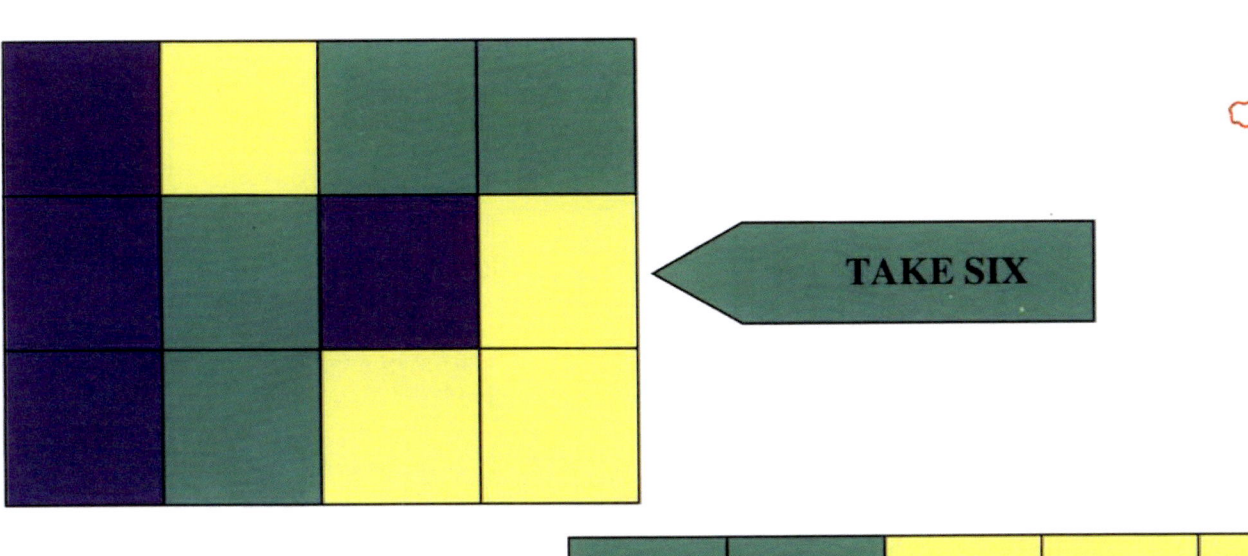

TAKE SIX

TAKE TEN

Pixel Design

The base of a cubical box is divided into 6 x 6 square pixels
and each pixel is either black or white.
From these four views into the box can you work out
the shape of the design on the base?

Use the 'Puzzle Proof Cut-out' from page 31 to verify your solution.

One in Eight

Only one of these coloured cubes could be made by folding
the net at the centre. Which one?

Seeing Stars

A network of blue lines divides the rectangle below into many differently shaped areas. In your mind's eye, can you see which areas to colour so that both of these two star-shapes appear?

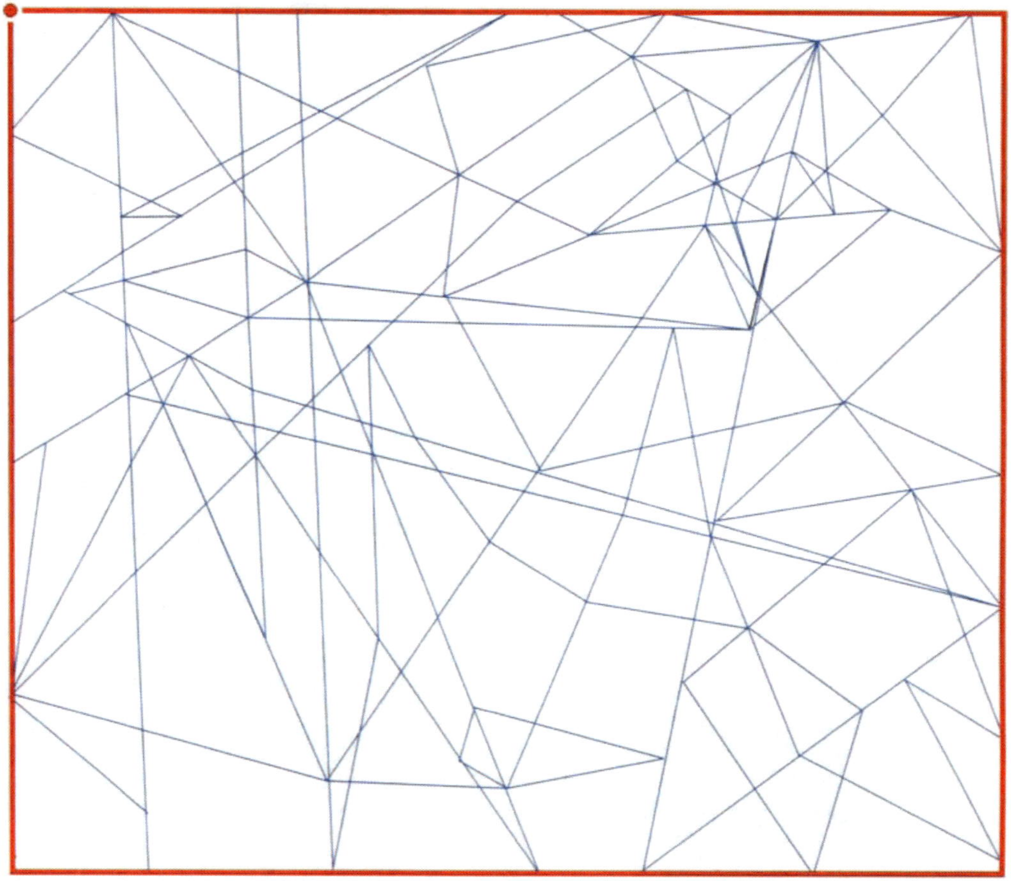

Use the 'Puzzle Proof Cut-out' from page 31 to verify your solution.

Odd One Out

Which of these shapes is different from
all of the others?

Exact Inverses

Each image of these three pairs should be an exact
inverse of the other, rather like positive and negative.
Black areas on one should be yellow on the other
and vice versa.
One of the three masks A, B or C, if placed
over the right hand image of each pair, will
make all the pairs into exact inverses.
Which one?

POSITIVE

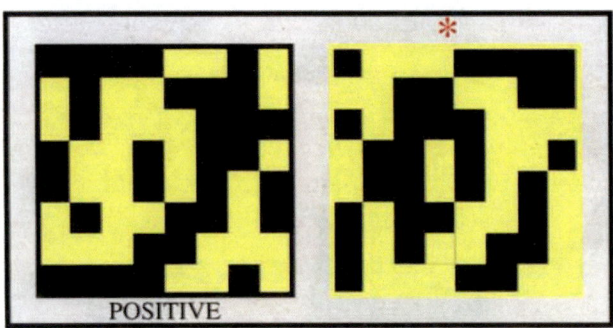

POSITIVE

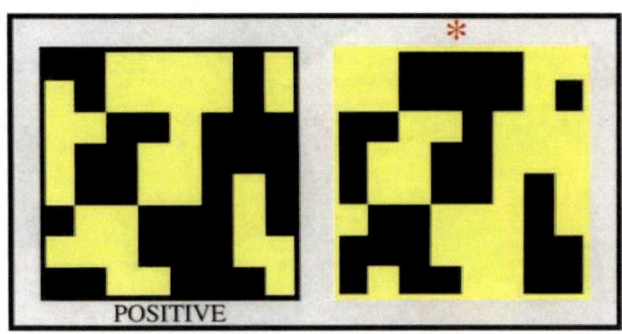

POSITIVE

A
WINDOW
NEGATIVE

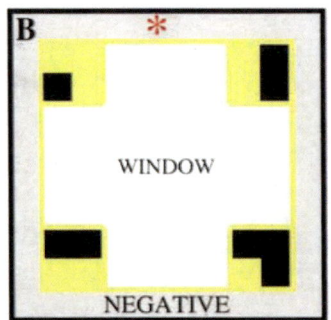

B
WINDOW
NEGATIVE

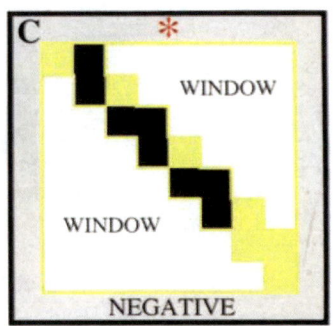

C
WINDOW
WINDOW
NEGATIVE

16   *Use the 'Puzzle Proof Cut-out' from page 31 to verify your solution.*

Through the Window

Through a cross-shaped window in a square mask, a number of coloured dots can be seen. In your mind's eye, can you decide which colour or colours can be seen in the window after moving the mask from its starting position up 14 units and right 30, then down 4 and left 6?

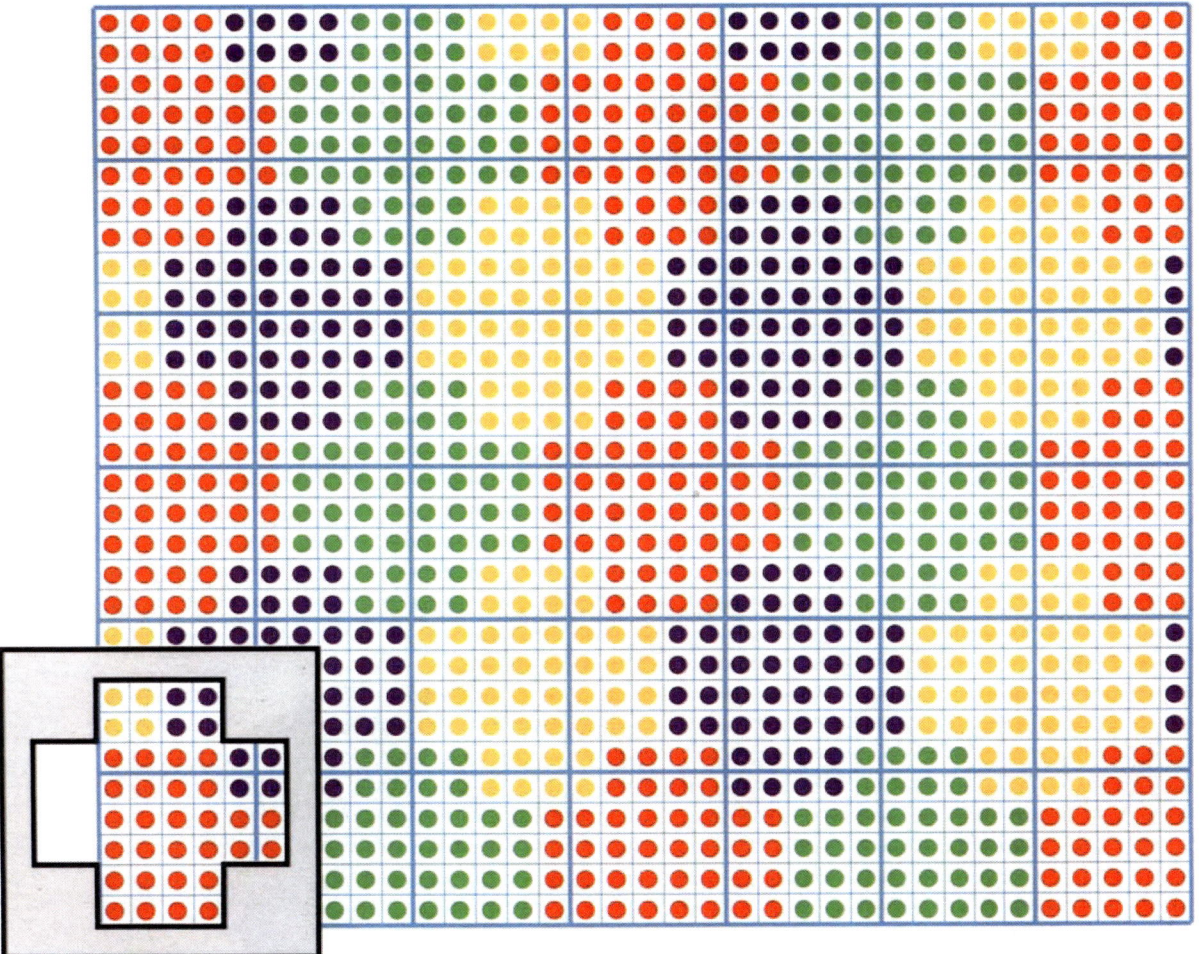

Use the 'Puzzle Proof Cut-out' from page 31 to verify your solution.

Equal Areas

The sum of the areas of each pair of touching semicircles is exactly equal to the area of one of the other single semicircles. In your mind's eye, can you work out which pair goes with which? What geometrical property makes it certain that the areas are precisely equal and not just roughly so?

Use the 'Puzzle Proof Cut-out' from page 31 to verify your solution.

Colour Clues

Eight pieces fit together to make a complete loop, but in this diagram
four of them have been moved out of position. In your mind's eye
can you put them back correctly? What makes this puzzle
especially interesting is that each piece contains a clue
about the position of some or all of the others.
Can you see what the clue is?

Use the 'Puzzle Proof Cut-out' from page 31 to verify your solution.

See Through

Imagine that each of these three tiling patterns has been printed on a piece of clear film.
In your mind's eye, can you reconstruct the pattern you would see if
all three pieces of film were placed exactly on top of each other?

Use the 'Puzzle Proof Cut-out' from page 33 to verify your solution.

Shortest Route

A collection of 28 measuring rods in centimetre lengths fit into a box 7 cm by 20 cm, so that there are seven rows and four rods in every row. One such arrangement is given below. In your mind's eye, can you find the shortest route from one edge of the box to the opposite one, travelling along the cracks? How long is this route? To make the diagram clearer, all the cracks have been widened, but assume that every side of every square is exactly 1cm.

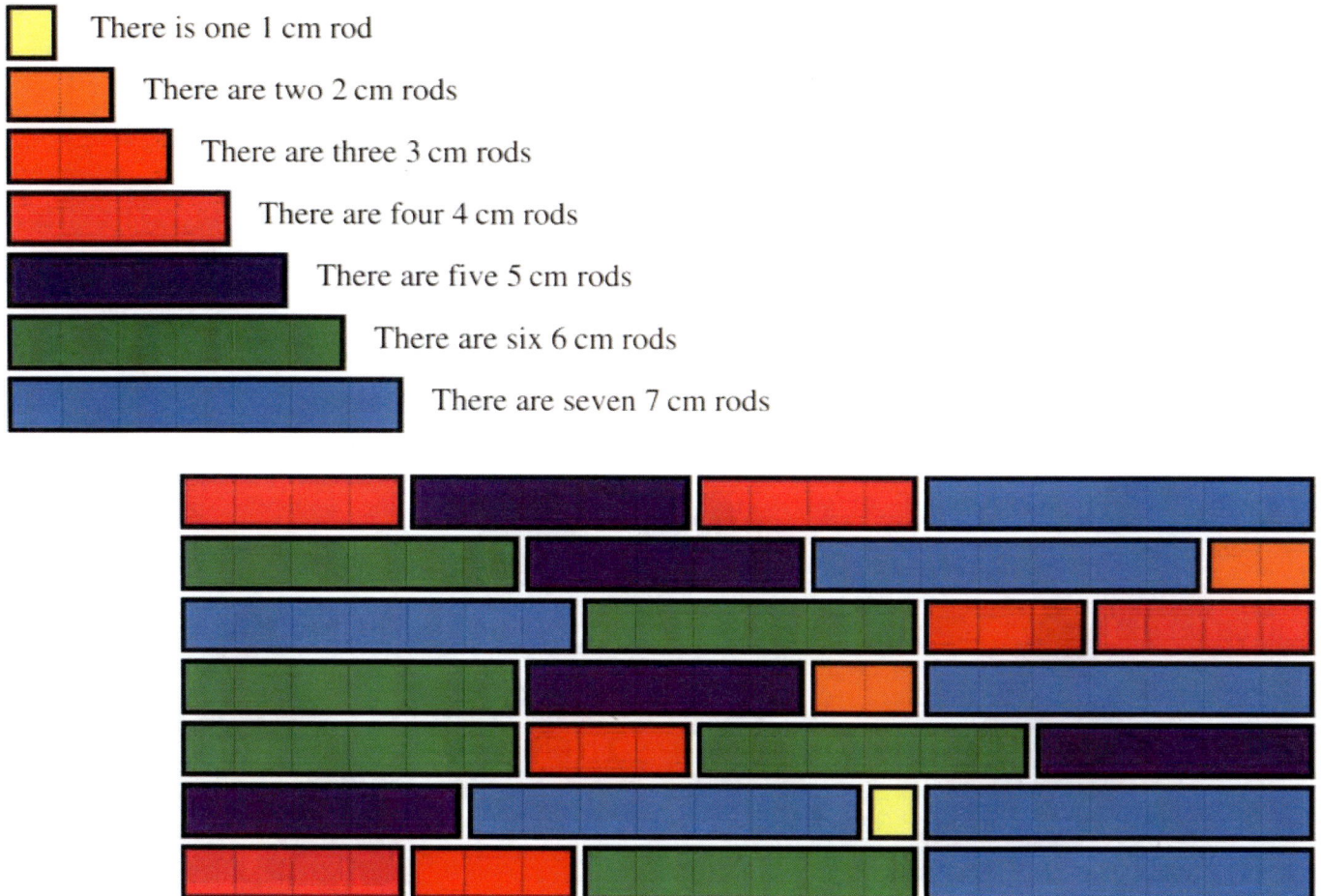

There is one 1 cm rod

There are two 2 cm rods

There are three 3 cm rods

There are four 4 cm rods

There are five 5 cm rods

There are six 6 cm rods

There are seven 7 cm rods

Use the 'Puzzle Proof Cut-out' from page 33 to verify your solution.

Pyramid Match

Each of the four nets A, B, C and D will fold up to make a tetrahedron, a pyramid with sides which are equilateral triangles. Only one of them can give both of the views below when placed in front of a mirror. Which one?

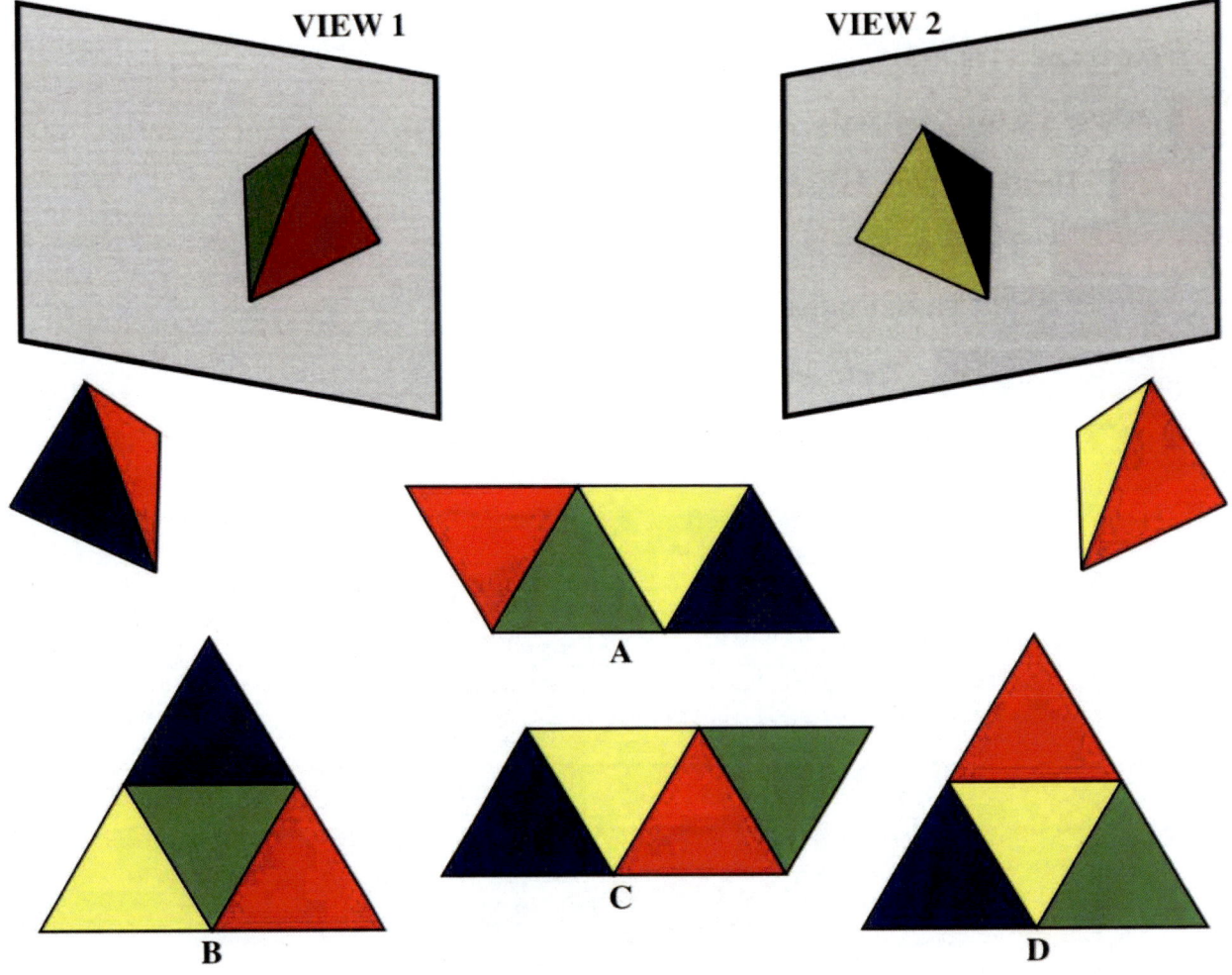

VIEW 1

VIEW 2

A

B

C

D

Use the 'Puzzle Proof Cut-out' from page 33 to verify your solution.

Lighting the Lamps

Three lamps and three batteries are arranged around a space for a triangular printed circuit board. In your mind's eye, can you work out which of the three boards A, B or C should be plugged into place so that all three lamps will light at the same time?

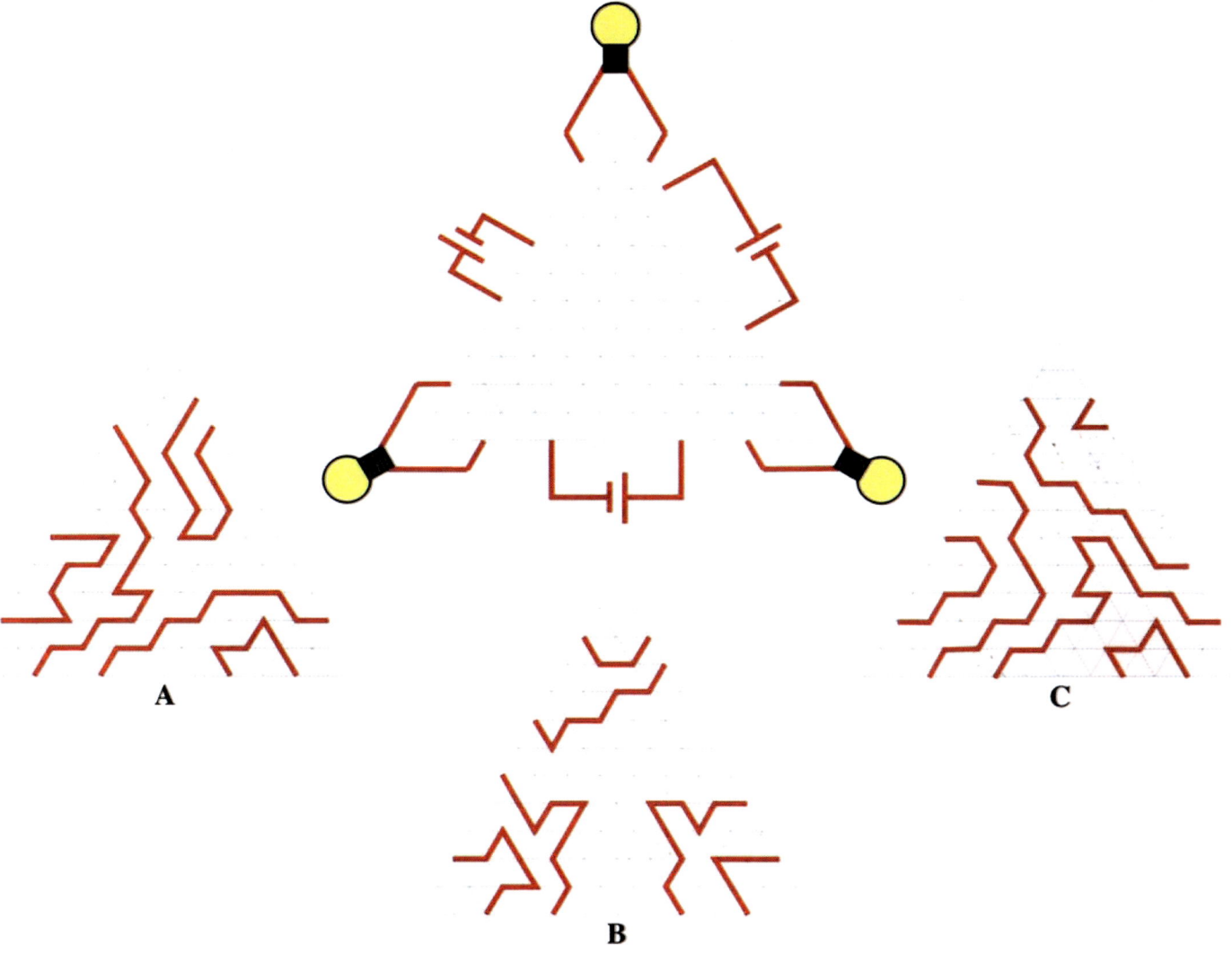

A

B

C

Use the 'Puzzle Proof Cut-out' from page 33 to verify your solution.

Curious Creases

Imagine taking a paper triangle which is blue on one side and orange on the back
and folding each corner to its neighbour and making a crease.
The three creases which this process creates appear to meet at a point.
Does this always happen whatever the shape of the triangle?

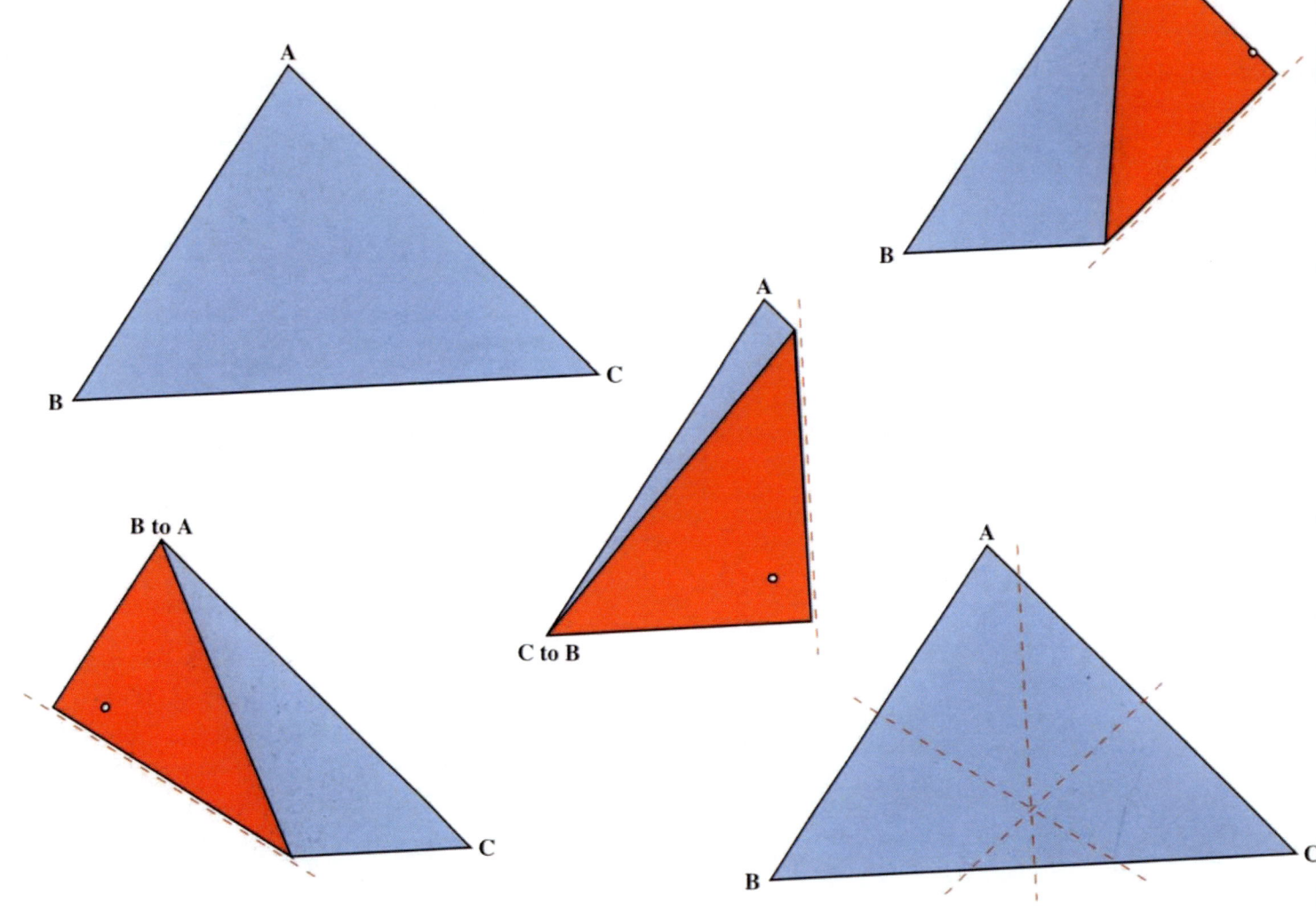

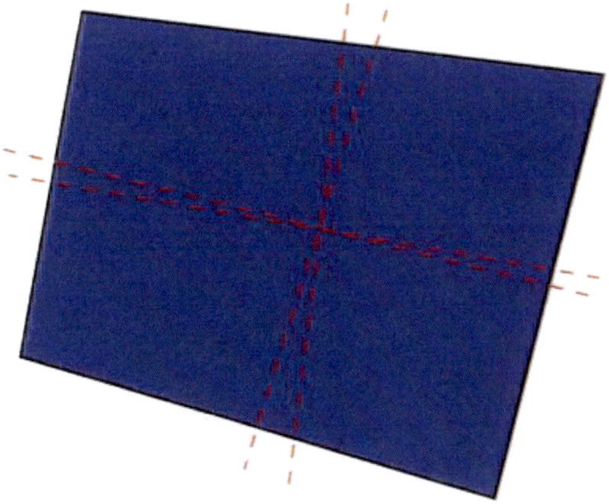

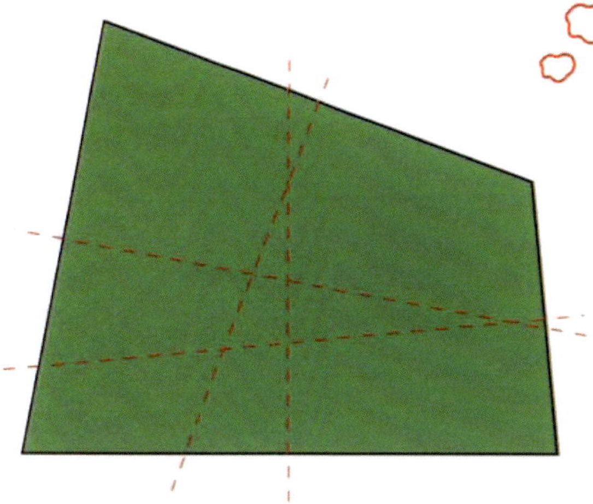

Now imagine folding a quadrilateral in the same way.

Sometimes this produces creases which meet at a pointbut not always.

Can you explain why this is?

Can you forecast what would happen to the creases on quadrilaterals A and B?

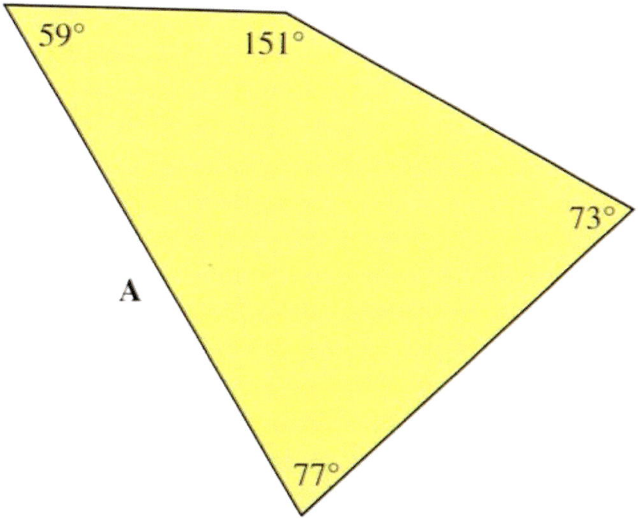

A

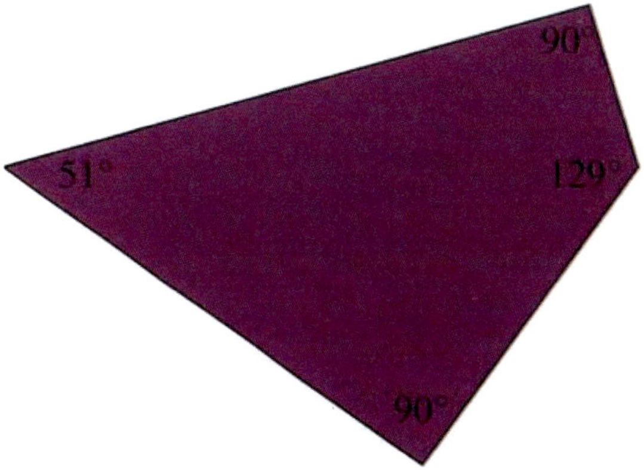

59°   151°

73°

77°

B

51°   90°

129°

90°

Magic Circles

It is appropriate that the final puzzle in this book is probably the hardest to visualise.
You have to imagine a model made from two pieces of paper, a base ring and a rotor.
Having cut out both pieces in your mind's eye, place the rotor on the base ring
and pass some of the rotor's dotted circles behind those on the base ring.

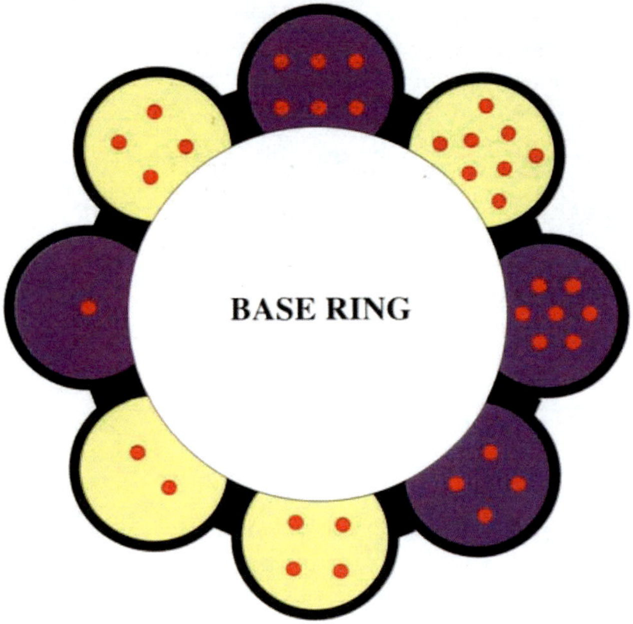

BASE RING

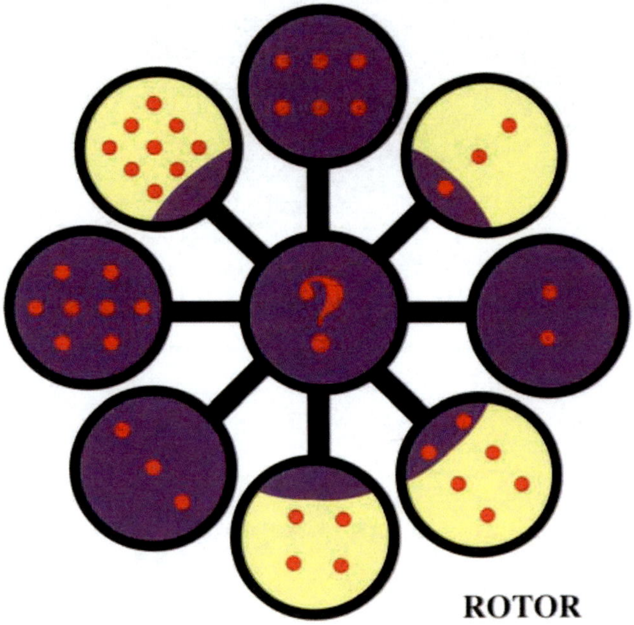

ROTOR

The puzzle is to position the rotor and
to choose which circles go under or over
in such a way that there are
15 dots in eight lines of three.

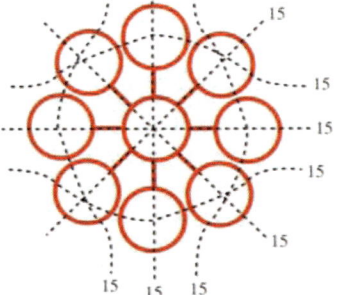

How many dots must there be at the centre of the rotor?

Use the 'Puzzle Proof Cut-out' from page 33 to verify your solution.

Puzzle Proof Cut-outs 1 & 2

Cut out these three pieces from this side

For Puzzle 2

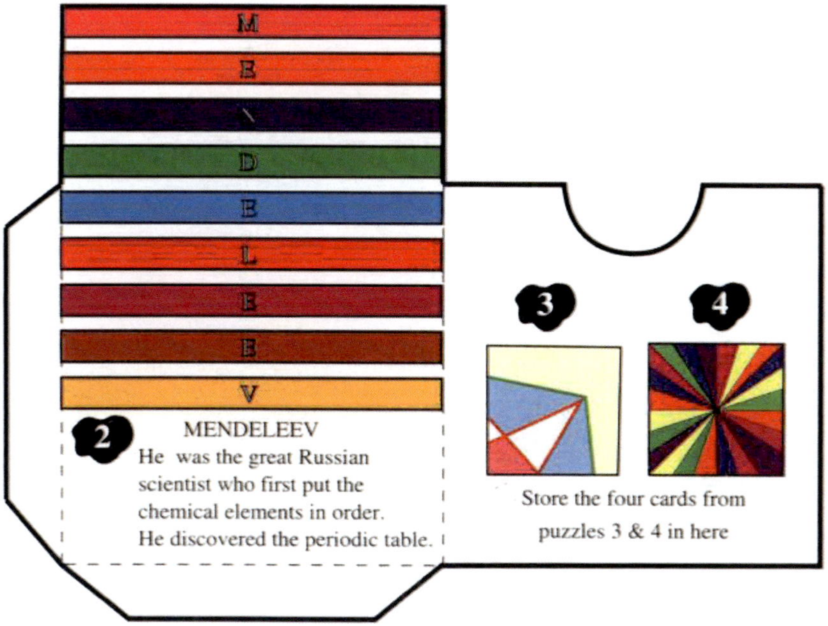

M
E
N
D
E
L
E
E
V

2 MENDELEEV
He was the great Russian scientist who first put the chemical elements in order. He discovered the periodic table.

3

4

Store the four cards from puzzles 3 & 4 in here

For Puzzle 1

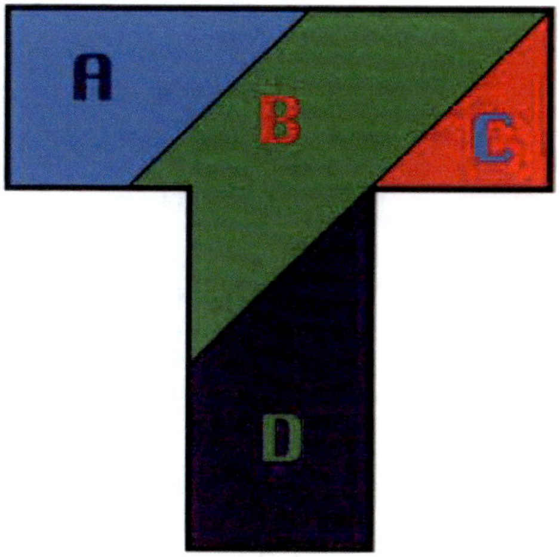

A
B
C
D

Cut out this pocket and glue it inside the back cover

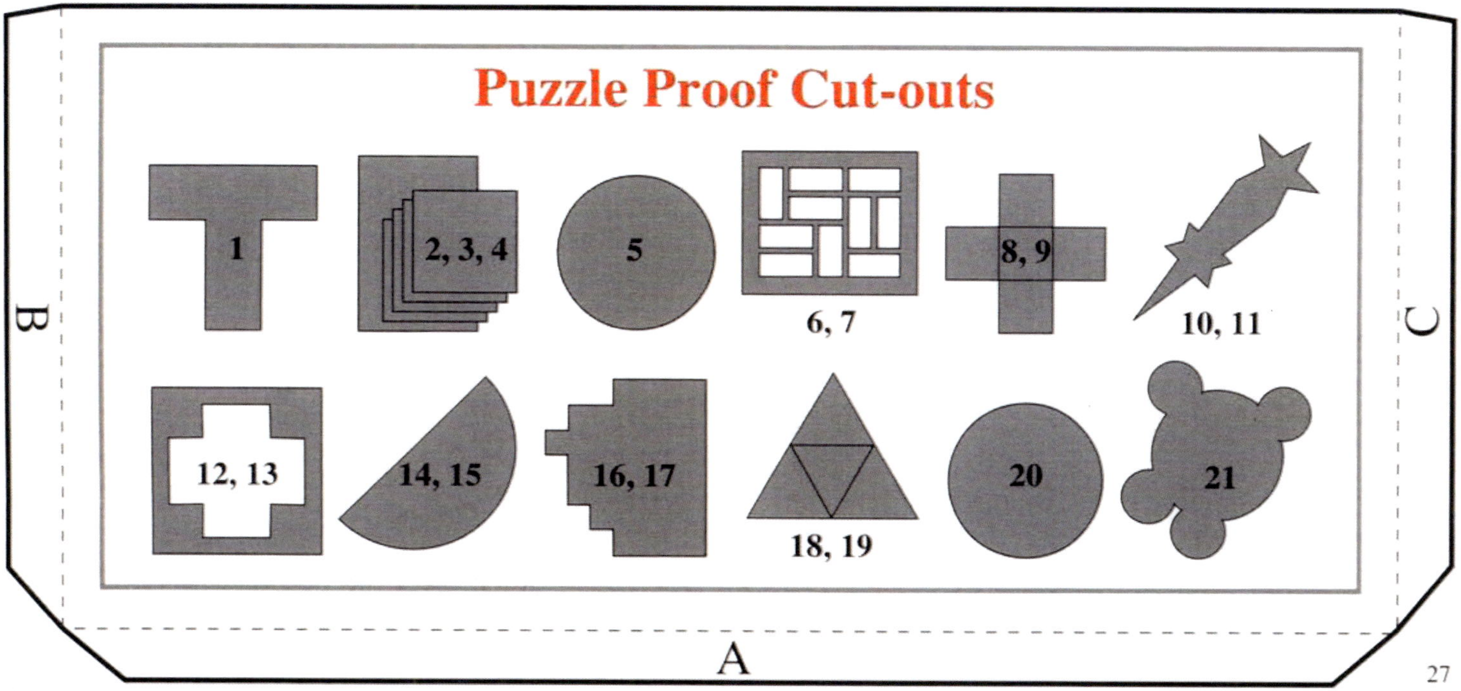

Puzzle Proof Cut-outs

B

C

1

2, 3, 4

5

6, 7

8, 9

10, 11

12, 13

14, 15

16, 17

18, 19

20

21

A

27

Cut out these pieces from the other side

This puzzle is a variation on the classic T puzzle designed by Sam Loyd. Try tracing the four shapes on to stiff card and you have the puzzle in its original form. Few people find it easy to make the T shape in spite of there only being four pieces.

1

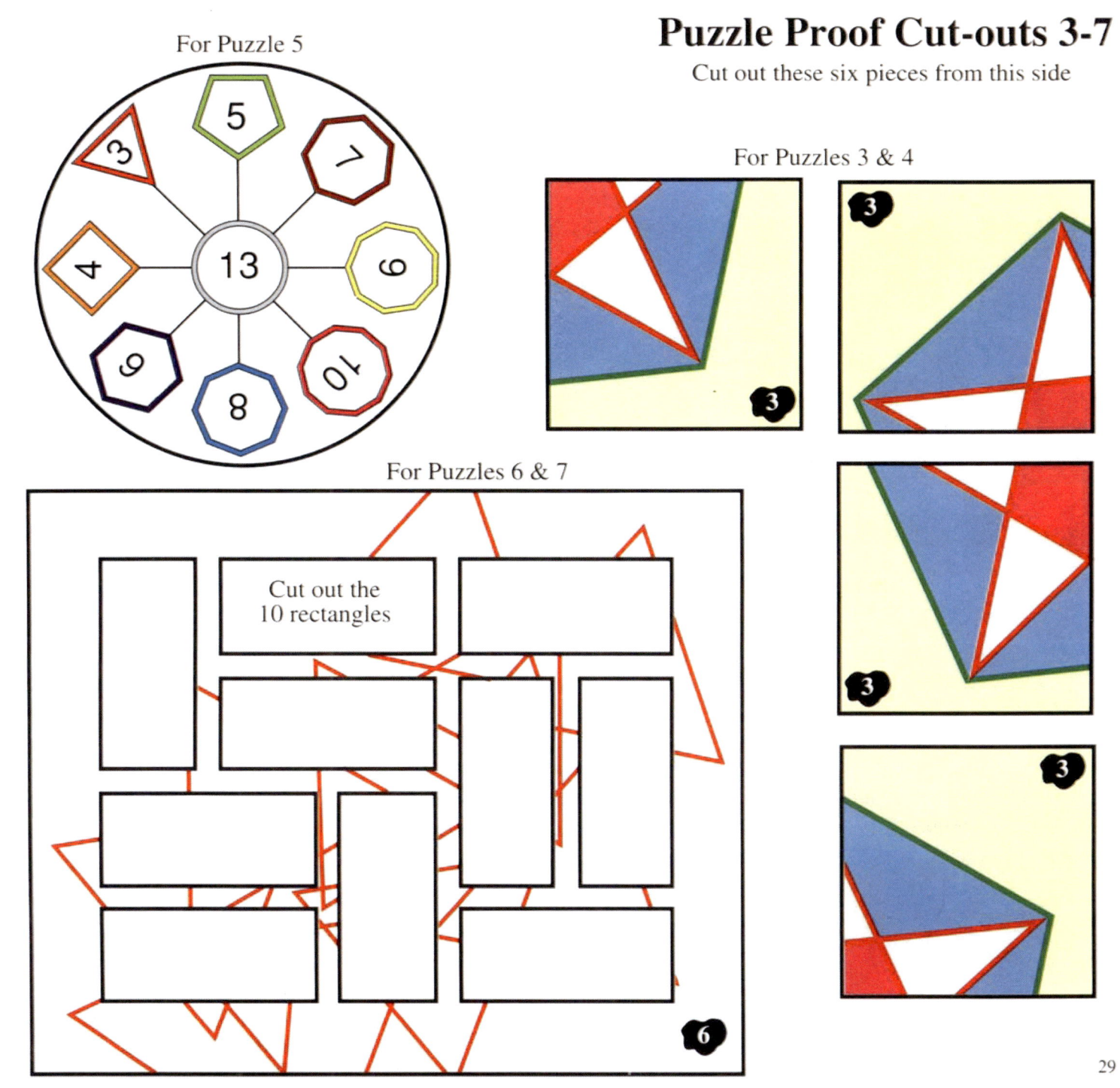

For Puzzle 5

Puzzle Proof Cut-outs 3-7

Cut out these six pieces from this side

For Puzzles 3 & 4

For Puzzles 6 & 7

Cut out the
10 rectangles

29

Cut out these pieces from the other side

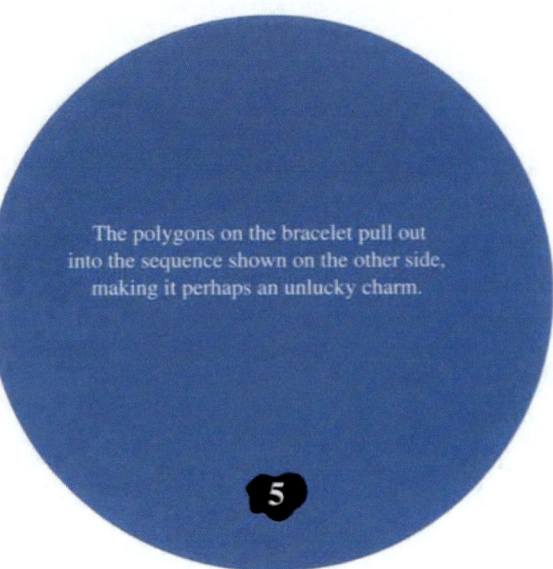

The polygons on the bracelet pull out into the sequence shown on the other side, making it perhaps an unlucky charm.

5

7

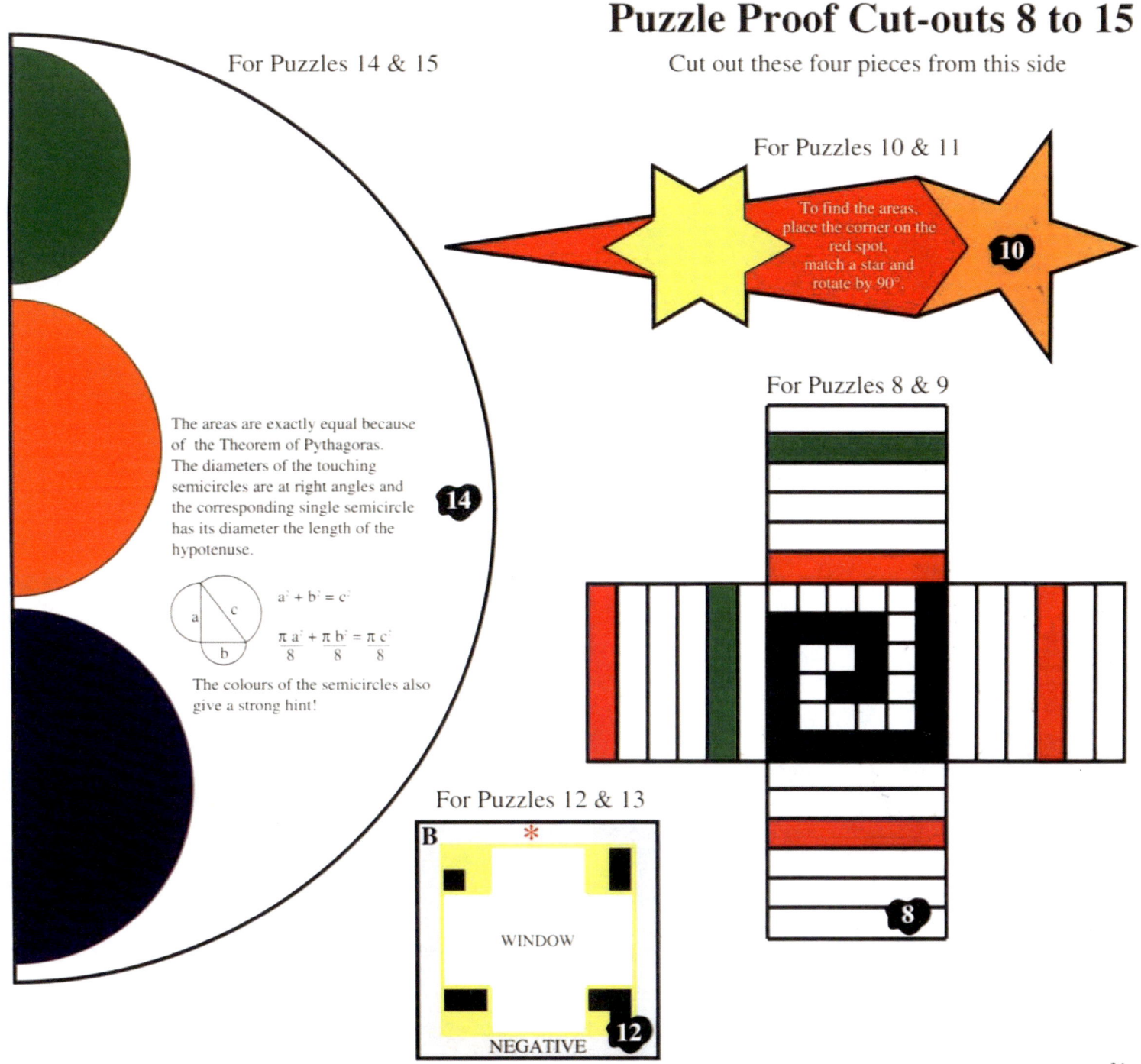

For Puzzles 14 & 15

Cut out these four pieces from this side

For Puzzles 10 & 11

To find the areas, place the corner on the red spot, match a star and rotate by 90°.

10

For Puzzles 8 & 9

The areas are exactly equal because of the Theorem of Pythagoras. The diameters of the touching semicircles are at right angles and the corresponding single semicircle has its diameter the length of the hypotenuse.

14

$$a^2 + b^2 = c^2$$

$$\frac{\pi}{8} a^2 + \frac{\pi}{8} b^2 = \frac{\pi}{8} c^2$$

The colours of the semicircles also give a strong hint!

For Puzzles 12 & 13

B

*

WINDOW

NEGATIVE

12

8

Cut out these pieces from the other side

COLOUR CLUE
Look at the first colour on each piece
as you move in a clockwise direction.

Cut out these four pieces from this side

For Puzzle 20

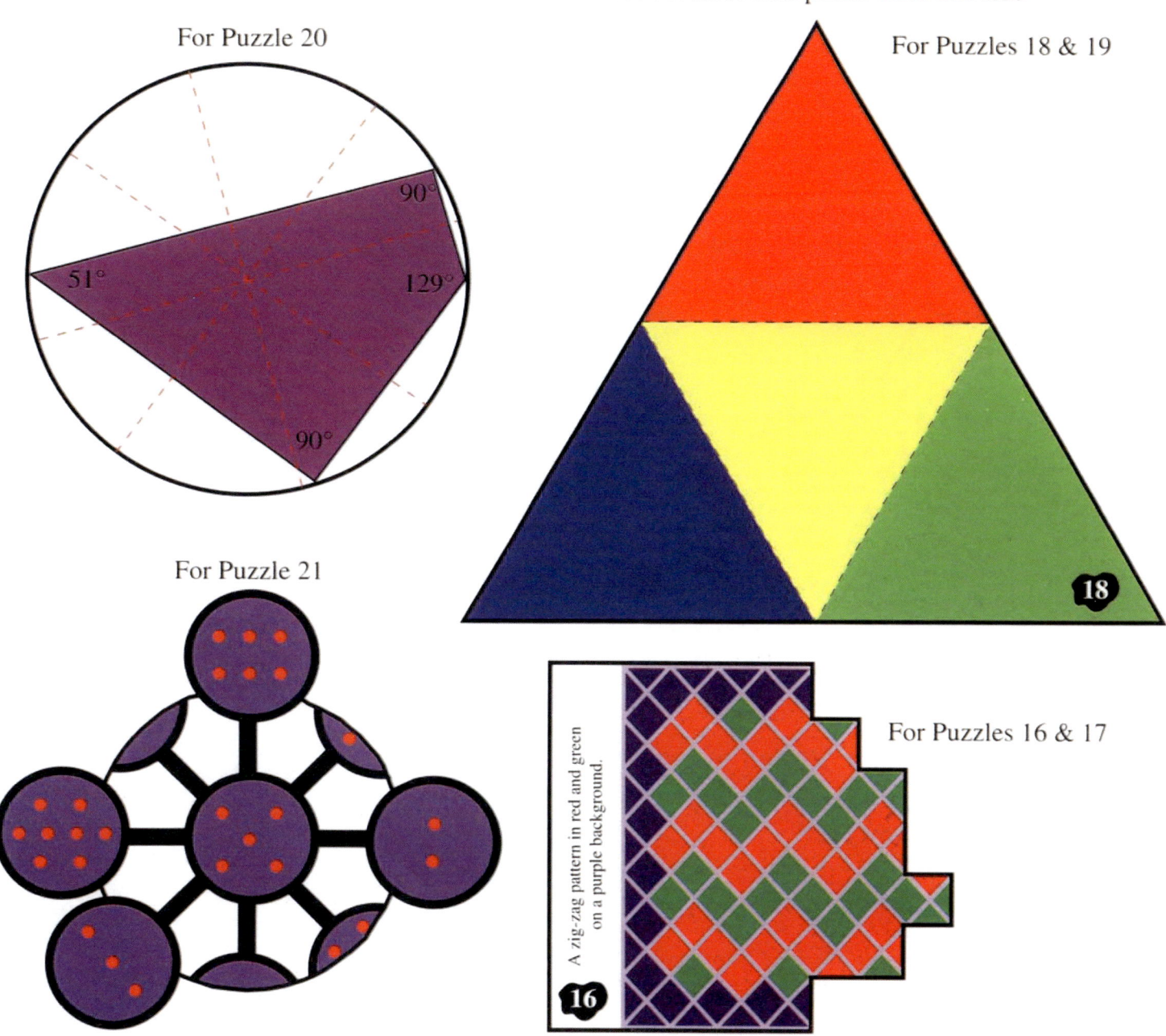

90°

51°

129°

90°

For Puzzles 18 & 19

For Puzzle 21

A zig-zag pattern in red and green on a purple background.

16

18

For Puzzles 16 & 17

33

Cut out these pieces from the other side

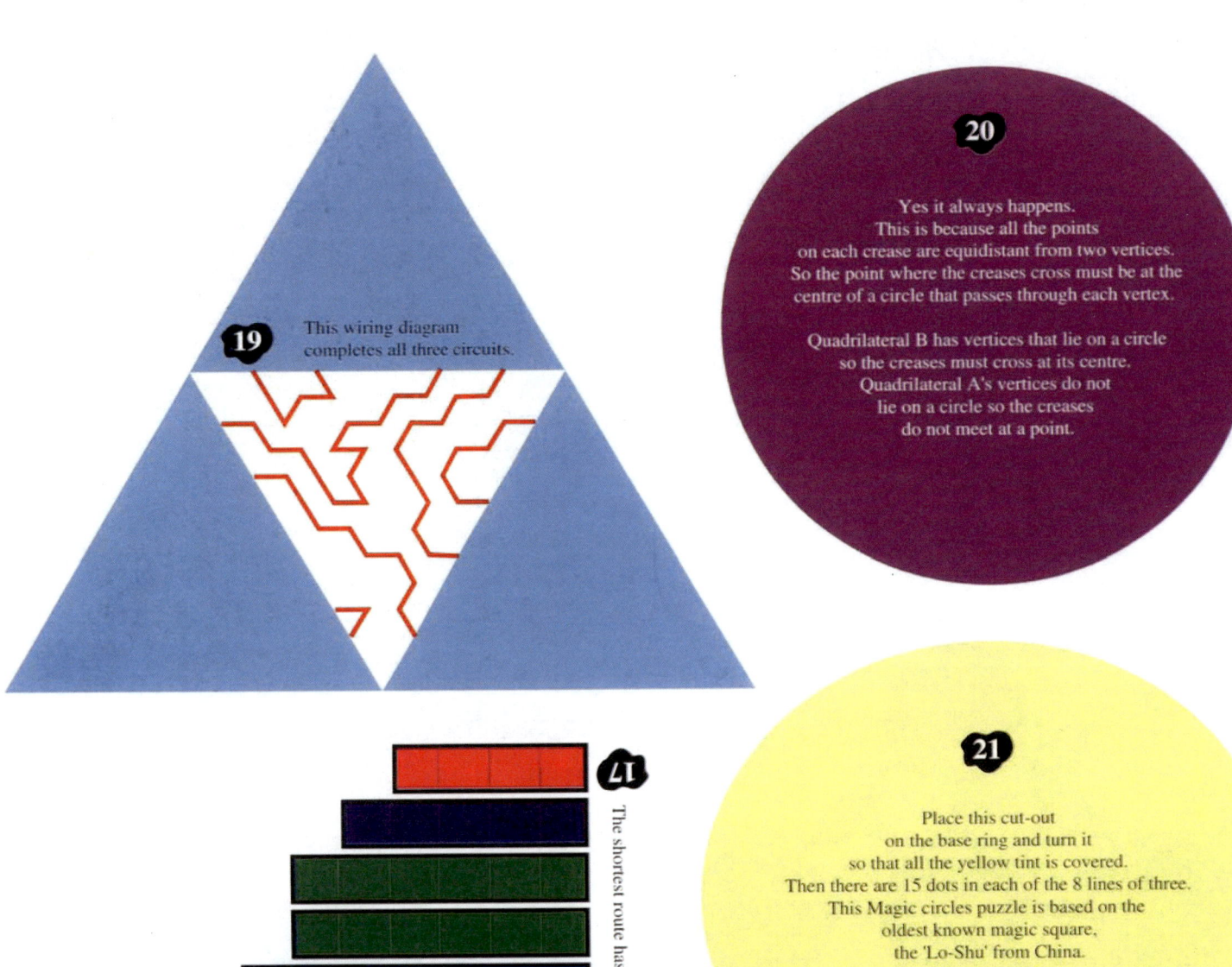

19
This wiring diagram completes all three circuits.

20
Yes it always happens.
This is because all the points
on each crease are equidistant from two vertices.
So the point where the creases cross must be at the
centre of a circle that passes through each vertex.

Quadrilateral B has vertices that lie on a circle
so the creases must cross at its centre.
Quadrilateral A's vertices do not
lie on a circle so the creases
do not meet at a point.

41
The shortest route has a length of 13 cm.

21
Place this cut-out
on the base ring and turn it
so that all the yellow tint is covered.
Then there are 15 dots in each of the 8 lines of three.
This Magic circles puzzle is based on the
oldest known magic square,
the 'Lo-Shu' from China.

8	1	6
3	5	7
4	9	2